MEET DEREK JETER

Baseball's Superstar Shortstop

Ethan Edwards

PowerKiDs press

New York

Published in 2009 by The Rosen Publishing Group, Inc.
29 East 21st Street, New York, NY 10010

First Edition

Editor: Amelie von Zumbusch
Book Design: Greg Tucker
Photo Researcher: Jessica Gerweck

Photo Credits: Cover, pp. 5, 6, 11, 12, 13, 14, 15, 16, 18, 20, 21, 22, 25, 26, 27, 28, 28 (inset) © Getty Images; pp. 9, 10 © Diamond Images/Getty Images; pp. 17, 19 © AFP/Getty Images.

Library of Congress Cataloging-in-Publication Data

Edwards, Ethan.
  Meet Derek Jeter : baseball's superstar shortstop / Ethan Edwards. — 1st ed.
      p. cm. — (All-star players)
  Includes index.
  ISBN 978-1-4042-4488-7 (library binding)
  1. Jeter, Derek, 1974– —Juvenile literature. 2. Baseball players—United States—Biography—Juvenile literature. I. Title.
  GV865.J48E39 2009
  796.357092—dc22
  [B]
                                        2008000884

Manufactured in the United States of America

Contents

Have you ever had a dream come true? When Derek Jeter was six years old, he told his parents that one day he would play **shortstop** for the New York Yankees. Guess what happened? Jeter's dream came true.

Today, Derek Jeter is probably baseball's most famous **athlete**. Many sports fans and sports **experts** believe that Jeter is one of the most clutch players of all time. A clutch player makes great plays when his or her team is in trouble. Jeter is also the captain of his team. The Yankees chose him to be their captain because he is a good leader.

The New York Yankees are the only major-league team that Derek Jeter has ever played for.

Shortstop is the position between second base and third base. It is generally considered the hardest fielding position to play.

The Kid from Kalamazoo

Derek Jeter was born on June 26, 1974, in Pequannock, New Jersey. When Derek was four, the Jeter family moved to Kalamazoo, Michigan. His parents, Charles and Dorothy Jeter, are **avid** baseball fans. Charles even played shortstop for his college baseball team.

Derek Jeter got excellent grades in high school. He was also the star of his high-school baseball team. He became famous at an early age. In Jeter's final year, the American Baseball Coaches Association, the newspaper *USA Today*, and the company Gatorade all named Jeter the high-school baseball player of the year. That meant he was the best high-school baseball player in the United States!

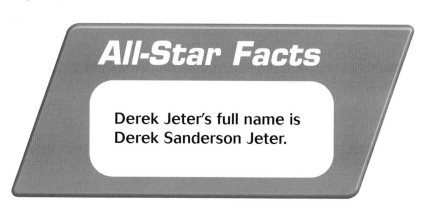

All-Star Facts

Derek Jeter's full name is Derek Sanderson Jeter.

The Minor Leagues

George Steinbrenner has been the owner of the Yankees since the 1970s. Steinbrenner followed Jeter's high-school career and thought highly of him. The Yankees **drafted** Jeter to play **professional** baseball when he graduated from high school in 1992. Jeter completed one year of college and then left to play professional baseball. He says that he hopes to go back to college someday.

Baseball players must prove themselves in the **minor leagues** before they play in the majors. The minor leagues are a system of baseball teams that allow players to **develop** their skills. Jeter struggled in the minors at first. He got nervous every time a ball was hit in his direction. In his first season, he made 56 errors. An error happens when a player fails to make an easy play.

In 1994, Jeter (left) and fellow minor-league player Carlton Fleming (right) practiced with the Yankees at spring training.

While he was in the minor leagues, Jeter worked hard to improve his skills. Here, he is practicing catching ground balls at spring training.

Jeter worked hard and improved. In 1994, sports **journalists** voted him Minor League Player of the Year. Finally, he seemed to be ready for the majors!

Rookie of the Year

Jeter played his first major-league games in 1995. However, he did not play well. The Yankees sent him back to the minors after only two weeks. Once again, Jeter worked hard to improve. He returned to the majors in 1996 and hit a home run in the first game of the season!

During his first full season in the major leagues, Derek Jeter hit a total of 10 home runs.

Jeter got along well with Joe Torre, the Yankees' manager. The head coach of a professional baseball team is called a manager. Torre became a **mentor** to Jeter. Torre helped Jeter deal with the pressure of playing for the Yankees.

New York City, the Yankees' home, is the biggest city in the United States.

Derek Jeter loves New York City and is very happy to play for the Yankees.

Joe Torre (right) and Derek Jeter (left)
continued to work well together until
Torre left the Yankees in 2007. They
remain friends.

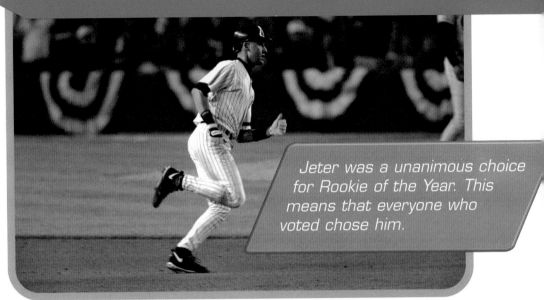

Jeter was a unanimous choice for Rookie of the Year. This means that everyone who voted chose him.

Yankees often find themselves in the spotlight. This creates a lot of **stress** for the players. Even great athletes have found it difficult to play in New York. However, Jeter just had fun playing. He could not believe he was lucky enough to play for his favorite team!

It did not take Jeter long to become a star. In 1996, baseball journalists named him **Rookie** of the Year. Jeter even helped his team win the 1996 World Series! The World Series is baseball's championship. Jeter had certainly done well in his first full season in the majors!

The Yankees' New Star

Every year he has played, Jeter has continued to make important plays and get important hits. The Yankees have reached the **postseason** every year Jeter has been on the team. Jeter helped his team win the World Series again in 1998 and 1999.

Jeter's great fielding skills helped the Yankees win the World Series against the San Diego Padres in 1998.

On October 13, 1999, Jeter made this great catch in the first game of the American League Championship Series.

Jeter had a great season in 1999. He had the second-best batting average in the American League. He also hit 102 RBIs in 1999. "RBI" stands for "runs batted in." This means that Jeter helped his team score 102 runs. RBIs are very important.

Jeter played for the American League All-Star team in 1998 and 1999. Playing for an All-Star team is one of baseball's highest honors. Every year, the best players from the American League and the best players from the National League are picked to form All-Star teams, which play against each other in the All-Star Game. Most baseball players never get the chance to play in the All-Star Game.

Jeter has played in many All-Star Games. Here, Jeter is laughing with Jorge Posada (middle) and Nomar Garciaparra (right) at the 2000 All-Star Game.

Derek Jeter made the thousandth hit of his career during the 2000 season.

Mr. November Does "the Flip"

The 2000 season was Jeter's best yet. He helped the Yankees win their third consecutive World Series. He also became the first player in history to win the All-Star Game MVP award and the World Series MVP award in the same season. "MVP" stands for "most valuable player." These awards mean that Jeter did more to help his teams win than any other player on the team.

Jeter (right) and fellow Yankee Scott Brosius (left) cheered after the Yankees won the American League Championship in 2001.

In 2001, Jeter made one of the most famous **defensive** plays in the history of baseball. The Yankees faced the Oakland Athletics in the postseason. It looked like Jason Giambi was going to score for the Athletics. Then, Jeter made

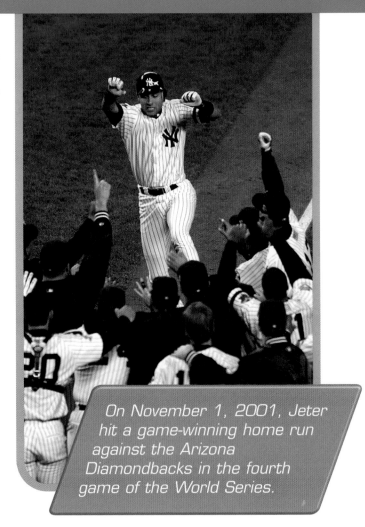

On November 1, 2001, Jeter hit a game-winning home run against the Arizona Diamondbacks in the fourth game of the World Series.

a stunning catch and "flipped" the ball to Yankees' catcher Jorge Posada. Posada tagged Giambi out and stopped him from scoring. The play is now known as "the Flip." *USA Today* ranks "the Flip" as the seventh-best baseball play of all time.

The 2001 World Series was **postponed** because of terrorist attacks on New York and Washington. This meant that major-league baseball was played during the month of November for the first time. Jeter hit the very first home run in November. This earned him the nickname Mr. November.

Though Jeter and the Yankees played well in the 2001 World Series, they lost to the Arizona Diamondbacks by four games to three.

Clutch in the Postseason

Jeter is considered to be one of the best postseason players of all time. Sometimes great players do not play well in the postseason or in important games. These players cannot handle the pressure. People call this choking. Jeter knows how to deal with the pressure. Joe Torre said that Jeter "handles the stress of this game as well as anybody."

Jeter does not choke. He actually plays better when the pressure is on. He enjoys it. Jeter holds the major-league records for hits and runs scored in the postseason. This is partly because Jeter has not missed a postseason yet!

One reason Jeter is such a clutch player is that he is both a good batter and a great defensive player.

The Yankees are one of the most popular sports teams in the world. Even people who do not follow baseball know Jeter's name. He is a huge **celebrity**. In 2005, *Forbes* magazine listed Jeter as one of the world's top 100 celebrities. Jeter has even appeared on the television shows *Seinfeld* and *Saturday Night Live*.

Jeter is so famous that he cannot cross the street in New York City without being recognized. Luckily, Yankees fans love Jeter. He signs as many **autographs** and shakes as many hands as he can. Jeter is shy, but he is polite to his fans.

All-Star Facts

Jeter does not have any pets because he is afraid of animals.

Derek Jeter attends many social events and awards shows. Here he is at ESPN's "NEXT" Party in 2003.

Jeter (right) often autographs baseballs, baseball jerseys, bats, and photos for fans.

Baseball is important to Jeter, but he knows there are more important things in life. He values family. Jeter's parents attend as many Yankees games as they can. Jeter always tries to spot his mother in the stands before each game so he can say hi.

In 1996, Jeter and his father created a **charity** called the Turn 2 Foundation. Turn 2 is a pun, or play on words. Making a double play, or a play that earns two outs for the other team, is called turning two. Jeter wears the number two. The Turn 2 Foundation encourages children and teenagers to turn to sports and academics instead of drugs and **alcohol**.

Along with Turn 2, Jeter supports other charities. For example, Jeter (right) appeared with Joe Torre (left) at an event for Torre's Safe At Home Foundation.

After over 10 years of playing for the Yankees, Jeter continues to be one of the most skilled and best-liked baseball players.

The Road to Cooperstown

Jeter's accomplishments will probably earn him a spot in the National Baseball Hall of Fame and Museum. This is a museum in Cooperstown, New York, that honors the history of baseball. Only the very best baseball players of all time make it to the Hall of Fame. Many other talented players are not quite good enough. However, Jeter is likely to be selected after he stops playing because he is already considered to be one of the best shortstops ever to play the game.

This will not happen for some time, though. Jeter is likely to play for his beloved Yankees for many more years.

One of Jeter's greatest plays is "the Dive." He made this difficult catch in a game against the Boston Red Sox on July 1, 2004.

Height: 6' 3" (1.9 m)
Weight: 195 pounds (88 kg)
Team: New York Yankees
Position: Shortstop
Uniform Number: 2
Bats: Right
Throws: Right
Date of Birth: June 26, 1974

2007 Season Stats

At Bats	Runs	Hits	Home Runs	RBIs	Batting Average
639	102	206	12	73	.322

Career Stats as of October 2007

At Bats	Runs	Hits	Home Runs	RBIs	Batting Average
7,429	1,379	2,356	195	933	.317

Glossary

alcohol (AL-kuh-hol) A liquid, such as beer or wine, that can make a person lose control or get drunk.

athlete (ATH-leet) Someone who takes part in sports.

autographs (AH-toh-grafs) Copies of a person's name, written by that person.

avid (A-vid) Eager or excited about something.

celebrity (seh-LEH-breh-tee) A famous person.

charity (CHER-uh-tee) A group that gives help to the needy.

defensive (dih-FEN-siv) Playing in a position that tries to prevent the other team from scoring.

develop (dih-VEH-lup) To grow.

drafted (DRAFT-ed) Selected for a special purpose.

experts (EK-sperts) People who know a lot about a subject.

journalists (JER-nul-ists) People who gather and write news articles for newspapers or magazines.

mentor (MEN-tor) A trusted guide or teacher.

minor leagues (MY-nur LEEGZ) A group of teams on which players play before they are good enough for the next level.

postponed (pohst-POHND) Pushed something back.

postseason (POHST-see-zun) The time after the regular sports season when play-off and championship games are held.

professional (pruh-FESH-nul) Someone who is paid for what he or she does.

rookie (RU-kee) A new major-league player.

shortstop (SHORT-stop) The baseball player who stands between second and third base.

stress (STRES) Worries.

Index

Web Sites

Due to the changing nature of Internet links, PowerKids Press
has developed an online list of Web sites related to the subject
of this book. This site is updated regularly. Please use this link to
access the list:
www.powerkidslinks.com/asp/jeter/